Princess Charming:

LOVE INSIDE OUT

By

Joe E. Sully

Title: Princess Charming: Love Inside Out

Author: Joe E. Sully

Layout and Cover: Joe E. Sully

www.bridgevisionllc.com

Library of Congress Catalogue-in-Publication Data is available upon request. Originally published: 2020.

ISBN: 9798589057461

To all the lovers of poetic words

out there.

Table of Contents

Introduction 10

Deep Love 16

Angelic Voice 20

Princess Charming 22

The Leap of Faith 31

Into You 33

Be Mine 36

Highway Encounter...................39

Before I Knew Her Name 42

Your Smile................................46

Magical You 49

From Head to Toe 52

When I Love You 55

Here I Am 58

Memories 62

My Mighty Queen 66

My Hearth Is Alive 69

Self-sacrificing Angel 75

Dillemma 79

Struggles 85

Only If 89

Please Don't Leave Me 92

The End of My Sunshine 96

Acknowledgments 103

About the Author 104

"Our greatest joy and our greatest

pain come in our relationships

with others"

Stephen R. Covey

Princess Charming:

Love Inside Out

Introduction

I would never consider myself a poet because I am not. I am a writer and a journalist who has tremendous writing experience, but I have not produced any poetry works until now. I have always wanted whatever I undertake to be done well. I have always been an avid reader of poetry, specifically those of my friend Jean Saint-Ville, PhD who have been sending me a poem, from Port-au-Prince, in French, religiously, every day for the past ten years. His passion for poetry got to my soul. Contagious! I have developed a large appetite for poetic words since. I enjoy reading poems. The desire to write poems had always been somewhere within me and I have finally conquered my hesitation.

Without hesitation, let me pose this question to you: What is the proper form of expression for our love of a friend, a soulmate or a life partner? Is there a universal way to be in love and express that love? Although there might be some standard answers to these questions, it is probable that each of us reading these words may have experienced some unconventional love situations during our existence. There are no barriers to love, it comes in all shapes and forms. They are all legit expressions of love, I assume.

In this short book of poetry, I share one or two poems that express my own experience of love (which is time and time again confused with lust). However, the majority of these poems are simply creations of my wondering imagination. I try to tell a story of lust, building relationship, love and sex in their different facets— the good and the ugly as I perceive them. The poems you are about to read are each a little piece of my lust, love adventure both imaginary and literal. The fantasy of love and the factuality

of it come alive through my
poems that I humbly tend you on
a silver platter, your majesty. I
hope you enjoy reading them.

16 | P a g e

Deep Love

L ove is entirely darkness

When my brilliance is

in distress

Love is all hope for the

hopeless

When She's really not the soulless

Love is wholly enlightening

When my darkness stops

lengthening

Love is more understanding

For Ms. Payne and Navarro

Love is help we are handing

For the time that we borrow

Love is all pain and sorrow

For the time we don't follow

Love is unconditional

And all is forgivable

Love is all provisional

And our life is winnable

Love is a walk in the park

Of two lovers of romance

Love is us leaving a mark

Of a life lived at a glance

Love is pure, sour and sweet

Love is help with no deceit

Love is choice with no retreat

Love is love with no beneath

Love is eye on the ball

Love is in fact the thing

Love is all, love is all

Love is all or nothing

Angelic Voice

I heard your voice, and it is truly sublime

Your sweet voice sounds like the wind in the palm

The waves of the sea don't move me like your voice

A magical voice for you, magical Noyce

I hear angels sing, you, entrance,
call my name

More than seraphs in heavens
your voice acclaim

The goodness of my warm heart
on bended knees

Hoping your voice will say: yes,
take my heart's keys

Princess Charming

A letter to my wife to tell
her in one line
She's the most brilliant
amongst all of them combined

Your supreme intelligence is
beyond skyline

You don't read minds, but you get
my sigh like road sign s

You grasp it all including my
silence, define

In real life, Einstein bowed before
your mind design

Is that why you boiled water and
it's flavorful?

And you feed me Massaman
curry, I'm grateful

Once you enter the kitchen, it's all
delightful

I don't deserve this; your skillful

hands make me full

Yes, because of your compassion

you dare to care

When it comes to take care,

there's no need to compare

You're the most genuine, my love

to you I declare

To me you're no cross to bear,

true, I want to swear

Everywhere you go, they call you professional

Boss says transactional, I say obsessional

Nail it again! then your boss calls you rational

Your standards put you on the map, it's national

For my dreams, and lost illusions, you're my helpmate

For my gleams and schemes,
you're my soulmate

Our hustles won't make neither
you nor I cellmate

Always we're teammates, there
won't be no cell-plate

Night and day, you're the same
force, busy as a bee

Now the girls next door, they
become your franchisee

You, Belle , becoming wealthy is a guarantee

Winkles on the face with age, you're no retiree

Your life's credo: fall seven times, stand right back up

Your strength seems too much for life's struggles to breakup

When all the flags are down low, I see you get up

No doubt, clearly your resilience
has no matchup

No need to mention how you
laugh at life sometimes

I'm stunned! How do you turn
failure into fun times?

I'm here with you like
cheerleaders at the half-times

Your presence is no mountains to
climb, it's pastimes

By the river, I catch your curves
under the tree

She's world class beauty "She," I
whispered, on my knee

That's your Princess Charming, a
little bird told me

When I asked for your sweet
hands, you told me: feel free

I was afraid you'd reply: not my
cup of tea

I then realize you're the only fish

in the sea

And I said to myself you'll suit me

to a T

The Leap of Faith

I'm that auk standing up there

Being pushed by my dad's gut

To jump now despite the height

The unknown of my short life

I'm that tern too scared to jump

Off the perilous, high cliff

Asking nonstop if the turf

Will smile large at first contact

I'm that boy, oh, so afraid

To take the step, leap of faith

To ask, please, if you don't mind

For the love of God be mine

Into You

When I see you, I see God's answer to my prayer

When I see you, I do speak in *"la langue de Moliere"*

When I see you, I see a large treasure to cherish

When I see you, I'm so ready,
even to perish

When I see you, I now want to
embrace fatherhood

When I see you, I spread the word
in the neighborhood

When I see you, I see us building
our empire

When I see you, I see a boss lady
in the right attire

When I see you, I see the only
fish in the sea

When I see you, I dream to join
our family tree

When I see you, each time I'd like
to say, "Yes, I do"

When I see you, each time I offer
myself to you

Be Mine

Be mine, until the end
of time

Be mine, you Ms.
Spices and Thyme

Be mine, and our bodies and souls
shall rhyme

Be mine, for there will be no
crime

37 | P a g e

Be mine, since it won't cost a
dime

Be mine, life's mountains we will
climb

Be mine, romance, love in our
prime

Be mine, to drink honey and lime

Be mine, let's do it all in mime

Be mine, I can shake-up your
grime

Be mine, may the world hear our chime

Be mine, ambitious and sublime!

Highway Encounter

On the highway I saw you, dancing girl

Joyful in your car, ivory tower

To me you smiled, then, I gave you a pearl

Every word I told you was a flower

Through the widows, I saw you all groovy

Through the widows, you gave me your number

We blocked the road like in a real movie

Suddenly, I became a burn rubber

I disappeared after you served muffin

For memories, I left only the fun

Our bond I didn't want us to toughen

Our short-lived promise was a hit and run

42 | Page

Before I Knew Her Name

Before I knew her name, I knew the charm of her touch and the taste of her wet tongue

Before I knew her mom and dad's name and declaim, I knew her curves, smell and exclaim

Before I knew her name, I
attended her celestial event,
playing with her half-moons in
the middle of the black space

Before I knew her position and
her life's mission, body extended
and relaxed, she made me learn
how to release

Before I knew her name, it was
quickly over between us, such a

strong flame in corn silk that dies
faster than lighting

Before I knew her name, I knew
her deep inside

Before I ate melon, she asked for
eggplant to slide

Before I knew her name, LORD!
she wanted to ride

Before I went below, she begged
me to make her fly

Before I knew her name, we both
changed like the tide

Before I said hello, we were both
saying goodbye

Before I knew her name, oh now I
want to hide

Before we end the show, she saw
the lies in my eye

Your Smile

I see diamonds only when to me you smile

When you smile, the sky is turned upside-down

I see myself strong even to go to trial

When you smile, I forget my own hometown

47 | Page

I see the end of my life, going in
style

When you smile, happiness only I
write down

I see my loads going fertile as the
Nile

When you smile, white falling
snow keeps eyes down

Your smile is my happiness just
like girl seeing diamond

Your smile makes me want to
change my name to Boss Don
Dimond

Your smile is as beautiful as the
Caribbean Sea, it is divine and

It makes me feel elevated,
enlightened and heightened

Magical You

Your eyes are like stars in
the sky at midnight
Your lips are the
sunshine of my day after dark

Your magical voice's sound makes
my heart and my phallus' head
dance without music

Your skin's tenderness is finer
than the velour that covers and
caresses my body softly

Your beautiful face is like my
paradise where roses of love grow

Your presence surrounds me like
the invisible but powerful wind

If you were mine, I wouldn't want
to go anywhere else, even to
heaven

If you were mine, I'd fallow the
trace of your love even to the dark
hell

From Head to Toe

I want your body more than dry land waiting for rain

From my spinning head, a dream of your beauty arose

I dreamed of you saying yes to my request to be obsessed

In my obsessed mind, I see myself loving you until seventy

I'm seventy, I can't stop loving
just like when I was a teen

At that time, I loved you from
head to toe, we were in love

I now love you, my little angel,
from head to toe

Of pure roses I will shower you
from head to toe

I will caress your body slowly
from head to toe

While licking milk, wine, honey
on you from head to toe

Hips, lips move as I touch your
body from head to toe

Arms, legs, mouth open, covered
with stars, from head to toe

From now 'til next time, your
body beeps from head to toe

When I love You

When I love you, I feel like a king on a throne

When I love you, I see a full moon at noon

When I love you, I see a bright sun at midnight

56 | Page

When I love you, I walk on stars
as my red carpet

When I love you, I see the river
running upstairs to the sky

When I love you, I'm covered
with upturned trees rooted in
heaven

When I love you, I face Goliath
only I walk tall, look him down so
little

When I love you, I'm fearless,
nothing in this life can ever block
me now

When I love you, I dream of all
your love, and loving you from
head to toe

Here I am

Here I am, tired, broken and lost without you

Here I am, this weekend offering the rest to you

Here I am, take all of me, yes—
my heart and my soul

Here I am, in your arms, feeling
that I'm truly whole

Here I am, in the rain, I don't
want to wait in vain

Here I am, ready to make the
jump and catch your train

Here I am, to love and cherish
you now and again

Here I am, body and soul, I'm
yours with might and main

Here I am, in your life, feel no
pain, I'm here to stay

Here I am, watching you smile—
my life I bring to bay

Oh darling, please make me forget
the wrong my exes have done to
me

Oh baby, please keep me in
chains, and make me your
prisoner for life

Oh sugar, please let me love you,
give our love immense happy
ending

Oh, my love, please forgive my
indecisiveness, now let's fly away

Memories

From a corner of my mind,
I found random memories
of you

The smell of Icewine tea on the
stove, bring back memories of you

Real dark roasted coffee in the
pot, bring back memories of you

A walk on the sand in South
Beach, bring back memories of
you

Picnic by the pond a summer day,
bring back memories of you

The scent of your body in my
arms, bring back memories of you

The very thought of you, sublime
you, bring back memories of you

Your memories disrupt my heart
and soul routine operation

I remember your touch, your
memories bring nervous
prostration

Your absence makes my heart
heavy with chagrin, what a
sensation

Thinking of you, miles away,
captured by fear and trepidation

Candle, photos in hands, I pray the Saints to save me from your starvation

Life's eraser will never erase you from my heart, dedication

Our love, sweet and sour memories, I'll sure keep on rotation

My Mighty Queen

When she walks that way, like a mighty queen

Her measured steps and body posture define elegance

The world's notorious mannequins fail into irrelevance

Like the falling leaves of an autumn scene

For me, life is inexistent, so I'll focus on the passage of a majestic wind

Tell me not I'm blind just because Queen Nadine's presence blows my mind

Her curves I deserve to calm my nerves, in the process of that life, I must preserve

My queen which my heart and
soul want to serve, for a magical
bond, we shall conserve

My Heart Is Alive

When all I want is you, despite you running away from

me

Well, that's good. My heart is alive

When all is pain and suffering
'cause your face, I can't see

Well, that's good. My heart is
alive

When night after night I'm losing
sleep over you, Queen She

Well, that's good. My heart is
alive

When to the whole world I say,
"Don't touch her, she is mine"

Well, that's good. My heart is
alive

71 | Page

When to hide my heart aching
and sorrow I go to wine

Well, that's good. My heart is
alive

When on my knees waiting for a
clear sign from the divine

Well, that's good. My heart is
alive

When everything is bleeding in
me, and my eyes see red

Well, that's good. My heart is
alive

When the lies and rumors about
us are being spread

Well, that's good. My heart is
alive

When my tight stomach and my
mouth forget the taste of bread

Well, that's good. My heart is
alive

When I want to follow you, even
to the dark hell

Well, that's good. My heart is
alive

When in despair I turn to things
like a Voodoo spell

Well, that's good. My heart is
alive

When being in your presence is
the only time I'm well

Well, that's good. My heart is
alive

Self-sacrificing Angel

The love you show me is wrapped with indebtedness

Is that why we're floating in an ocean of connectedness?

You give to me abundant love as if you were *Catherine de Médicis*

Is that why I don't feel the need
to go anywhere else, not even
East?

You filled my life with your
goodness for the sake of my
happiness

Now I'm stuck on you and, oh
goodness, I like that kind of
stickiness

Sometimes my mind wonders if you ever consider your own self-interest

In face of your self-sacrificing nature my agitated mind you bring to rest

In my life, I have a self-sacrificing angel that loves me more than her own self

I feel complete with your filling
love, my little angel, I do love you,
for yourself

All I want is to love you back, love
you back to the moon, more than
the stars

You make me feel like a superstar,
like a true Don smoking many
Cuban cigars

Dilemma

I found a love, oh it's truly beautiful and sweet

I found you, you the woman who took me off the street

I found a life-partner, my helpmate, I feel complete

I found an altruistic soul, never I won't cheat

It's the drama queen I'm running
from

Yes, that's the reason I pray with
psalm

It's the man-breaker I'm hiding
from

Stress you give me, make me go to
rum

I found a love, boy! She is nice
and easy and sweet

I found a love; she cares and
always makes sure I eat

I found the love that satisfies my
body with heat

I found you, you changed the
course of my life of defeat

It's your deceit that led me to
Rome

SOS! Oh Lord, I can't keep calm!

It's true, your affair with Uncle
Tom

Assess it, how much is it worth,
Noam?

I found a love that's elegant,
eloquent and sweet

I found the love I shall proudly
announce in a Tweet

I found a love I cherish from head

to toe; it's neat

I found a love more voluptuous

than a Royal Suite

It's all those exes listed in tome

Guess I'll wait until the cows

come home

It's four kids, four dads that made

me roam

Mess, way to see you with fine
tooth comb

Struggles

When stumbling blocks come on our love adventure way

Deep in my heart, a big part of me fades away

When night after night my soul doesn't sense your presence

My bones, and my aching heart
lose their essence

When traitorous doubts come to
paralyze you with a stun

To you my heart responds, I had
my run, baby I'm done!

When at times my future full of
unknown scares me to death

My clever mind runs to you, in
your company stays in depth

When your world is stealing you from me, leaving me alone in my zone

I scream, "Hold on to me, we're better together as one on our throne"

When the miles keeping us apart are killing me inside like a wronger

I see me on my way to be with
you until the end, growing
stronger

When the clashes of egos mixed
up with misbelief, poor talk seems
with no end near

The million reasons to love and
cherish, the very thought of you
makes our path clear

Only If

If the sea could talk, it would say how much tears I shed in it

When I think of you and cry, you're gone forever and always

If the cloud could stand alone and dance, oh I would dance with it

When our favorite music is on

and you're not in the hallways

If the trees could move like a pen

between my fingers, I'd write

When reading your love letters,

becoming a poet in love with you

If sunshine and flower could

cohabite, I'd swear to unite

When my heart refused to make a

pact with the devil in you

If the river, the rain and fire could

go back to their source

When all is said and done, with

you I'd start over new and fresh

If nature could shrink, I'd envelop

myself with its wonderous warps

When your empty, cold heart left

me without the warmth of your

crèche

Please Don't Leave Me

Please don't leave me,
please don't leave me my
love

What sense does my life make
without you?

Please don't leave me, please don't
leave me my love

What is the world worth without
we two?

If I'm a college you're the only
Dean

If our love life's a game, I'll go all
in

I'll create a kingdom where you'll
be queen

I'll share everything with you like
a good twin

Please don't leave me, please don't
leave me alone

Please don't leave me, please don't
leave me hanging

Please don't leave me, please don't
leave me hungry

Please don't leave me, please don't
leave me to die

I'll give the rainbow's colors for a
kiss

I'll serve you caviar for breakfast
in peace

I'm on my knees praying you for
a feast

I'm at war for you fighting like a
beast

I want to protect you like a High
Priest

I swear to cherish you, to say the
least

The End of My Sunshine

When suddenly I am alone, it's when all went dark in the sunshine state of mine

Like Thor's hammer hitting my chest, I heard my heart jumping of rage inside of me

When you are nowhere to be
found, although in pain, my heart
I beg to set you free

At my lofty place of stay in the
City of Light, in my eyes all is
misery and ugliness without you

When our love's rivals finally stole
you from me, alas! Our unified
hearts and souls had become two

To stop being fooled, it took more
than one deceit before I saw what
I was getting myself into

When my sunshine went away,
was the day my loving heart
plunged into darkness in The
Sunshine State

At this turn of events in our
adventure, I refuse all options but
to submit my case into the hands
of fate

When the offspring to me
whisper, "Advise please;" to them
I shall insist firmly to never ignore
the sign

My aching heart is bleeding tears
of pain and sorrow

What happens to our magical
bond I thought was sacred?

My ever-curious mind is
becoming plain and narrow

What happened to our, "Would
you marry me, Sunshine?" Non-
sacred?

My flesh is burning with desire
for more of your outgrow

What happened to, "Yes, I do take
the place in your heart,
semisacred?"

To them, my optimistic, hopeful heart only sings life of a sweet adventure

Sublime creature of my sunshine state, we'll be back for a great future

Love always comes back, with the same intensity, sometime different head, different names

Your sun rises on my life, and
now what remains are sublime
memories of two hearts' flames

103 | Page

Thank you to all of you love spreaders out there making the world a better place. Much love and affection!

About the Author

The author, Joe Eriland Sully is a United States citizen who emigrated from the city of Port-au-Prince and has lived in the United States for some time. There, he has been invited as a guest speaker to talk about Haiti, which he has traveled from north to south and east to west. Founder and president at

Bridgevision Production, LLC, he is the author of the books *Surviving America: From the Bench to the Podium* and *Heroes in the Wake of Haiti's Catastrophe.*

Joe is a journalist, a survivor and a witness of Haiti's earthquake on January 12, 2010. In 2006, he began his journalistic career at the newspaper *Le*

Nouvelliste, the oldest daily in Haiti. He was employed afterward by the agency Haiti Press Network (HPN) and the newspaper *Le Matin*, the second oldest newspaper in Haiti, as a reporter and editor responsible for the *Portrait* (biography) section of the newspaper. In July 2011, Excel Institute of Communication and Journalism honored Joe with the "Certificate of Excellence" award for proven outstanding professionalism in the practice of journalism in Haiti.

Joe studied Journalism, Business Administration and Hospitality Management at Excel Institute of Communication and Journalism in Haiti, Central Piedmont Community College, East Carolina University and

Trinity Washington University in the United States.

www.ingramcontent.com/pod-product-compliance
Lightning Source LLC
Chambersburg PA
CBHW072103150726

47999CB00005B/1859